The Inner Work of Lent

A Journey With:

Helen Keller
Dietrich Bonhoeffer
Simone Weil
Martin Luther King, Jr.
Mother Teresa
Jesus of Nazareth

by
Phillip Cover and Donna Mollenkopf

ISBN 0-9763897-0-3

Printed in USA

Inner Work Books
4007 Longmoor Circle
Phoenix, Maryland 21131

Book design and graphics by Aziza L. Doumani

Dedication

To Irma Lauber, my mother,
whose life and memory inspires me in many ways.

To my parents,
Berwyn & Hilda Cover,
who were among my best spiritual teachers.

CONTENTS

Forward i

Acknowledgements ii

Abouth The Authors iii

Preface iv

PART I 1

1. The Journey to Jerusalem 3

2. Discerning God's Purpose 5

3. Losing Life to Find It 7

4. Taking Up Your Cross 9

5. Dying and Rising 11

6. Forgiving and Reconciling 13

7. Surrendering with Trust 15

8. A Journey with Six Remarkable Companions 17

9. How to Use The Journal 18

PART II

10. Beginning The Journey 23

11. First Sunday of Lent 29
A Week with Helen Keller
A Personal Reflection

12. Second Sunday of Lent 39
A Week with Dietrich Bonhoeffer
A Personal Reflection

13. Third Week of Lent 49
A Week with Simone Weil
A Personal Reflection

14. Fourth Week of Lent 59
A Week with Martin Luther King, Jr.
A Personal Reflection

15. Fifth Week of Lent 69
A Week with Mother Teresa
A Personal Reflection

16. Holy Week 79
A Week with Jesus of Nazareth
A Personal Reflection

17. Epilogue: Easter Sunday 87

FORWARD

Throughout my life I have been blessed with spiritual companions but it's only recently that I have learned what to call them. These are people who have walked attentively by my side and have listened carefully to what I do and do not say. They have asked questions that invite me to contemplate the meaning of my life in Christ and they have challenged me to open myself to God's Holy Spirit at work through me.

The writers of this Lenten resource have been such companions. They have reflected carefully on their own journeys of life in faith as well as on the world in which we live. They have honed their ability to catch glimpses of God's power at work and to assist others who wish to see more clearly. They understand that a spiritual journey isn't about information to be mastered, but rather about providing space in our lives, hearts, and minds for our God to speak.

Through this volume—a book and journal—they invite us to join them on a Lenten pilgrimage. Quiet time for meditation is organized around traditional themes of the Christian faith. They have asked some 20th century saints to meet us along the way so that we can learn from their experiences and perspectives what it means to live a faithful life in today's world. This wonderful weaving together of the Lenten themes with the wisdom of the saints beckons us to explore the ways in which the old story of faith creates new life within us. I have come to believe through this journal that this exploration will encourage and empower us to become more fully the people who God created us to be.

This journey is a worthwhile one in any season, but it is a special gift during Lent, when Christians for centuries have focused on Jesus' journey to the cross. As we walk with Jesus on his way to and through death, we pray that this book and journal will help us to follow Him. We do so trusting that we, too, can be filled with new life by the same power that raised Jesus from the dead and that the Spirit of Christ's resurrection can come alive within us. By God's grace may it be so.

Grace and peace,
Marie C. Jerge
Bishop
Upstate New York Synod, ELCA

ACKNOWLEDGEMENTS

There are always companions who travel with us on new paths in our journey. As we were writing this journal, there were a number of people who prayed and sat with an early version of this work, as part of their Lenten spiritual practice. Their encouragement, prayers, and support were a source of creative energy and grace as we moved through a number of revisions. We hold them in our hearts with deep affection and gratitude.

In making this endeavor a reality, we were blessed with the editorial guidance of Albry Montalbano who reviewed the work several times and offered specific and thoughtful suggestions about clarity, grammar, style, and mechanics of language. The thoughtful reviews and practical suggestions offered by Carolyn Matthews also facilitated our thinking and clarified our writing. Their contributions have greatly enhanced the quality of our efforts and so we acknowledge their gifts with love and appreciation.

We wrote this journal from a deep sense of trust that the same God who loves and guides us led us in this creative endeavor. We give thanks for the way God has brought us together in a work that invited us even deeper into the journey of Holy Week and into the lives of others who served as models for us.

ABOUT THE AUTHORS

Phil Cover is an experienced educator, priest, and former federal government executive. He also serves as a spiritual director, retreat leader, and pilgrim guide to the Sinai and New Mexico deserts. His spiritual roots are in the contemplative Christian tradition, from which he tends to the transformative work of the heart. He is co-author of *Journey with Purpose*.

Donna Mollenkopf is a former public school principal and area superintendent who currently directs a graduate program in education. A wife and mother, she considers all aspects of her life to be ministry and deeply values the contemplative practices of prayer. She is an active church leader, spiritual companion, retreat facilitator, pilgrim guide, and adult educator. She is a co-author of *Journey with Purpose*.

PREFACE

Over the centuries, Lent has become an intricate mix of religious and cultural beliefs, traditions, rituals, and practices. In more recent time, the focus of Lent has shifted from Lenten practices as an individual achievement to a renewed emphasis on the individual being changed and reshaped by the grace of Jesus' suffering, death, and resurrection. The word Lent comes to us from the Anglo-Saxon word lencten, meaning "lengthen," referring to the lengthening of days occurring in early spring. For Christians, it became the season of forty days of spiritual renewal, beginning on Ash Wednesday and ending on Easter Sunday. In their historical context, these forty days recall for us the time Jesus spent in the wilderness before beginning his public ministry. The centerpiece around which we focus the spiritual practices of Lent is God's unrelenting love for us manifested in Jesus' passion, death, and resurrection.

When we think of Lent, the words, concepts, and images that first come to mind are those that may have some negative overtones, such as repentance, sacrifice, suffering, passion, and death. Other Lenten notions have more positive implications, like, conversion, forgiveness, reconciliation, compassion, and healing.

Traditionally, the observance of Lent has involved fasting, praying, and performing works of charity. While these observances demonstrated actions for observing Lent, they were understood to be rooted in prayer and linked to Jesus' suffering and death. Fasting represented a form of body prayer; the act of praying itself lifted the concerns and desires of the heart to be one with the desires of God's heart; and works of charity were a form of active compassionate prayer for those in need. Over time, these practices developed into broader rituals of self-denial and penance. For some, they became an end in themselves, rather than a way of open and willing participation in the paschal mystery. These practices also took on the nuances of personal atonement, evolving into notions of individual worthiness and holiness, and the mistaken notion that if one worked hard enough, one could earn, merit, and deserve a heavenly reward. Fortunately, we live in a time in which there has been a shift back to a deeper awareness that what we understand as growth in the spiritual life is all God's work. Both the awareness and the growth are pure gift and absolute grace, wholly unearned, undeserved, and unmerited on our part. The overarching personal focus of Lent's forty days has also shifted back to the Gospel imperative of change and conversion, a real transformation of our mind and heart modeled on Jesus' life, teachings, death, and resurrection.

The focus of this Lenten journal as a spiritual practice is on Jesus' decision to journey to Jerusalem and the consequences of that decision, which ultimately led to crucifixion. The journal is structured around Jesus' specific insistence that we follow in his footsteps.

Part One

The Journey to Jerusalem

Most of the major decisions we make in life come from a deep place inside. No significant life decision—marriage, divorce, job change, adoption, geographic move—stands alone or on its own. These life-altering decisions are spiritual events. While we are consciously aware of the preparation needed to make a life-altering decision; there is also something beyond our awareness, something inexplicable and mysterious at work influencing our choices. We call this element "mystery." It is resident and active in us as grace and linked to God as the origin of our life. Life-altering decisions represent a convergence of many factors and considerations working together, sometimes without a coherent rational pattern, to become a life-altering, spiritual event.

Jesus' resolve to go to Jerusalem[1] is a life-altering, spiritual event rooted in love. In making this decision, Jesus insists on involving us. How? When he predicts that he will suffer, be rejected by the religious authorities, be killed, and on the third day be raised up,[2] Jesus connects his prediction to a mandate, "anyone who wants to be a follower of mine, let him renounce himself and take up his cross every day and follow me."[3] He also joins this to a consequence, "anyone who does not take his cross and follow is not worthy of me."[4] Jesus invites each of us to step into his life altering experience and participate in it by taking up our cross as he did—with love for the sake of love.

Jesus' decision to go up to Jerusalem is a journey within the journey of his public ministry and the larger journey of his life. "Jesus knew . . . he had come from God and was returning to God."[5] His resolve and the various factors that were at work within him shaping his decision, as well as the consequences that flowed from it, are inextricably bound together. They meet and form a single, cohesive event that continues to be at work within him until his death on the cross.

In the same way, we are challenged to see the significant decisions we make in life and the consequences that flow from them not as temporary, disconnected events, but as opportunities to redirect our energies so as to live life like Jesus.

ONE EVENT WITHIN A CONSTELLATION OF INTERACTIVE MOVEMENTS

To better understand this decision-event and appreciate the nature of our participation in it, we need to view it as a dynamic process, that is, a progressive, ongoing movement of six interconnected activities. These interior movements do not occur in a linear sequence, but unfold in a fortuitous fashion for our spiritual good. Within any major decision-event, one movement may seem to dominate for a while; at other times, several movements will be functioning together in unison; and sometimes two or more may overlap in parallel motion. However operative these six movements are, they coexist and continue to unfold in both known and mysterious ways.

The manner in which these movements are alive in us may best be likened to a statement from Jesus' conversation with Nicodemus. "The wind blows wherever it pleases; you hear its sound, but you cannot tell where it comes from or where it is going. That is how it is with all who are born of the Spirit."[6] Thus, the transformative work that is occurring within us is not of our making. We cannot simply, by an act of our will, make transformative change happen. Transformative change is the work of the Spirit in us. It is through our willingness to take up our cross daily, that these six interrelated and interactive movements become operative in us in ways we sometimes know, but more often do not.

These same "workings of the Spirit" were active in the whole of Jesus' life. The scriptures disclose that his conception was by the Spirit.[7] His childhood was summed up in the Christian scriptures this way: "The child grew to maturity, and he was filled with wisdom, and God's favor was with him."[8] At Jesus' baptism, the Spirit descends upon him, and thereafter he is "led by the Spirit through the wilderness"[9] to be tested. When Jesus begins his public ministry, John the Baptist points out to his followers that God gave Jesus "the Spirit without reserve."[10]

We will draw from Jesus' teachings in the gospel narratives and name these six interactive movements as: (1) discerning God's purpose; (2) losing life to find it; (3) taking up your cross; (4) dying and rising; (5) forgiving and reconciling; and (6) surrendering with trust. These six interior movements form the framework of our Lenten journey. To step into this life-altering experience is to undertake a journey of the heart, wherein we yield to the creative, transforming work of the Spirit in us.

Discerning God's Purpose

The Spirit wishes to engage us at the core of our personalities . . . the gradual drawing of the whole personality into the orbit of God's active presence and the realignment of all its faculties to the purpose of God.

Robert Morris[11]

Jesus' journey begins with a deep commitment, a vow to fulfill God's purpose for his life as he grew in his understanding of it. "I have come from heaven not to do my own will, but to do the will of the one who sent me."[12] To ensure that his followers clearly understood this, Jesus likens the will of God to food, the essential ingredient to sustain life. "My food is to do the will of the one who sent me and to complete his work."[13] Doing the will of God was not his mission alone; he extends it to all who follow him. If we commit ourselves to carrying out the will of God as Jesus did, the result is a deep personal relationship with God—"anyone who does the will of my Father in heaven, he is my brother and sister and mother."[14] Additionally, those who do the will of God are assured of eternal life. They will enter the kingdom of heaven.[15]

The process of discerning God's purpose is a process that begins and ends in prayer. While the process of discernment frequently involves choices, it would greatly over-simplify the process to suggest it is a matter of making a choice from among several available options. In reality, it is a much more complex endeavor in which we are looking at the alignment of the desire of our heart with the desire of God's heart for us. It involves prayerfully differentiating between competing goods, working though the pros and cons of alternatives that may be confusing and obscure or appealing and obvious. As we sift through what seems to be God's purpose for us, our passion for it, as well as our resistance to it, we need to find appropriate ways to test the promptings of our heart. Discernment may require a season of prayer, a time for the longings of God's heart to ripen in us, all the while asking: *How would*

You have me be with this? What would You have me do? In the Garden of Gethsemane, we find Jesus surrendering his very life in prayer to the will of the Father. He went away a second time and prayed, "My Father, if this cup cannot pass by without my drinking it, your will be done."[16]

❖

On Monday of each of the six weeks of Lent, the quote and question seeks to draw you into a deeper awareness of God's purpose for your life. You will move through different layers of discernment, exploring various dimensions of your life and to what extent they are aligned with God's desire for you.

❖

Losing Life to Find It

We seem to have, each one of us,
two selves warring within the one person.

Bishop Desmond Tutu[17]

At the heart of the spiritual life is a paradox about losing and finding life. Matthew's Jesus states, "Anyone who finds his life will lose it, and whoever loses his life for my sake will find it."[18] What precisely is the life I must lose, and what is the life I must find? Jesus himself struggled with this question when he was led by the Spirit into the desert to be tested. Through the journey of forty days and forty nights, he wrestled with the seduction of evil spirits who sought to persuade him that his true identity and happiness could be found in domination, power, and wealth. In the end, he rejected the seduction, finding and claiming his true identity in God.

For centuries ever since, Christians and others have sought to understand the meaning and implications of the paradox of losing life to find it. The austere asceticism of the second and third century desert mothers and fathers, the rules of monastic and religious communities that followed, and the reformation movements throughout the centuries in large part reflect the various ways of grappling with this paradox.

In the writings of Thomas Merton and others, we find the term "false self" referring to the life we must lose, and "true self" as the life we must find. In similar fashion, Paul in his Letters urges us to put off our "old self" [false self], which is being corrupted by its deceitful desires and to put on the "new self, created to be like God."[19]

Within this framework, the false self is the illusionary self we have worked hard to create and believe we are. The current slogans of "pull yourself up by your boot straps" and "be all you can be" suggest something of the cultural underpinnings of this self-created image we have fashioned for ourselves and will defend at all costs. The center of the false self is the ego; the center of the true self is life in God. We possess a false self and true self simultaneously. To shift the center of one's life from self to God may call for a significant change of heart. It will require a dismantling of our attachments and a stripping away of our addictions, because they are impediments to finding our life in the Source of Life. Our true self is a mirrored reflection of God's Very Self in us. Our true self is the self that existed in the heartbeat of God's love before each of us was breathed forth by Love into life. We simply need to rediscover it. The nature of our true self, our deepest and most authentic identity is found in these words spoken to Jeremiah. "Before I formed you in the womb I knew you, before you came to birth I consecrated you."[20]

❖

The quote and question for reflection on each Tuesday of the six weeks of Lent invite you to consider the paradox of losing life to find it in light of who you are and what you believe about yourself as well as your awareness of who you believe God is in relationship to your life.

❖

Taking Up Your Cross

Each of us is to take up our own lives in their wholeness to "carry our crosses" (respond to what is given), to love God and one another in whatever situation we find ourselves.

Elaine M. Prevallet, SL[21]

The mandate "take up your cross daily and follow me" is not meant to be one of simple imitation, because once we take up the cross we are powerless to carry it to its conclusion on our own. What is asked of us is the willingness to take up the cross daily. The rest is grace. We may wonder whether the cross chooses us or if we somehow choose our own cross. Regardless of how a cross comes to us, we need to name what it is that comprises the cross we carry and/or what is it we feel we are nailed to.

We refer to a number of experiences or conditions as being a cross, for example, a physical suffering, a psychological burden, a social economic hardship, a situation of perplexing uncertainty, or circumstances that are beyond our control. Some of these conditions are imposed upon us unwittingly like a serious accident or a grave illness. Other situations seem to evolve into becoming a cross as when we inherit the consequences of others' wrongdoing. Some crosses are of our own making, such as the results of poor choices or the outcomes of deliberate willful behavior. Taking up a cross can change our life in significant ways. Jesus would have us willingly embrace it with the same motivation of love with which he took up his cross. We embrace a cross differently when we take it up with love than if we accept it with resentment. Love can lessen the weight, softens the pain, and even mitigate some of its conditions. Love transforms the heart; resentment hardens it.

In coming to terms with the invitation to "take up your cross," some may wonder whether they in fact have a cross to carry. It may be that the invitation for them comes in a way in which they are being asked to share in carrying someone else's cross, like Simon from Cyrene who was pressed into service to help carry Jesus' cross.[22]

❖

Each Wednesday of your Lenten journey, you will consider Jesus' mandate of taking up your cross. You do so in light of the cross both as mystery and as the icon of unconditional love. The quote and question on each Wednesday seeks to move you beyond a focus on self and the question—why me, to the cross itself and the challenging question—*in taking up my cross what is love calling forth from me?*

❖

Dying and Rising

Every birth is a kind of dying. Every new stage of growth calls for letting go of what went before it. And this letting go hurts.

James Finley[23]

To bear fruit, a seed must die. To be transformed, we must die. While it is natural for us to resist what the process of dying calls forth from us, dying is crucial to growth in the spiritual life. Again it is all God's work, and we call it the paschal mystery. To teach us what this process of dying involves, Jesus uses two metaphors, one of the seed, and the other of the vine and the branches.

Of the seed, he said: "Unless a grain of wheat falls to the ground and dies, it remains only a single grain; but if it dies, it yields a rich harvest."[24] His listeners knew that every seed contained in itself its own future. They also knew that in order for the future of each seed to be realized, it had to be planted in the tomb of the earth. In the earth a deep, transformative mystery unfolds. The outer protective shell of the seed yields to the workings of the soil around it and dies. Inside the seed itself a new life begins to emerge, springing up through the soil to be nourished by the sun, water, and heat, causing roots to develop and to take hold in the rich soil, feeding the life within and above. This metaphor is a rich symbol of the activity of the paschal mystery that is at work in us.

Another metaphor that symbolizes the dying and rising process is that of the vine and the branches. Jesus equates himself with the vine, designates us as the branches, and God as the gardener who prunes the branches so they will bear even more fruit. Pruning can be an unpleasant experience as God is removing from us what is non-essential to our life in God. The work of pruning connotes a process of "emptying," sometimes referred to by the Greek word *kenosis*. It is an ongoing, thorough process whereby we are dismantled, stripped, and emptied out of what hinders us from living life fully in union with God.

We cannot experience the mysterious power of dying and rising with Christ unless we are willing to be changed, to let go of certain behaviors or ideas in order to experience a new life-giving good that is of far greater value than what we have let go of.

❖

The quote and reflection question for each Thursday of your Lenten journey invite you into a deeper acceptance of *kenosis* as a movement not of your own making, and the willingness of giving yourself over to truly being emptied out, of letting go, of dying, in order to receive abundant gifts of grace, freedom, and new life.

❖

Forgiving and Reconciling

By its very nature, reconciliation means committing ourselves to the hard and sometimes tortuous task of speaking and doing the truth in love.

Mary Ann Fatula, OP[25]

Forgiveness and reconciliation brings us in touch with our own heart and God's heart as few other things do. Forgiveness and reconciliation are acts of deep compassionate love. Notwithstanding the direct or indirect causes that call for forgiveness and reconciliation, they point to human brokenness and severed relationships that beg for healing, restoration, and love. Every need we have to be forgiven confronts us with our own capacity to hurt or inflict pain on others willfully or unintentionally. Conversely, our need to forgive others brings us face to face with the truth of our inner wounds, vulnerabilities, brokenness, and the causes of them.

For Jesus, forgiveness and reconciliation are deeply rooted in his motivation and resolve to go to Jerusalem and they become an important aspect of his teachings. Forgiveness is central to our relationship with God and others. Jesus teaches us to forgive as God forgives; and unless we forgive others, God will not forgive us.[26] On the cross, Jesus models his own teaching, "Father, forgive them, for they do not know what they are doing."[27] Reconciliation is so important to an authentic relationship with God that if we have a grievance with our brother or sister, we are to leave our gift at the altar and go to them and be reconciled before returning to the altar.[28] In the Christian system of beliefs, Jesus' suffering and death on the cross are the means in and through which humankind is reconciled to God, restored to original goodness, freed from the slavery of sin, and liberated from the power of death.

Forgiveness and reconciliation begin and end with God's grace. The process of forgiveness and reconciliation awakens within us as a conscious choice of our mind and a desire of our heart. Once we yield to grace and make the decision to release the person who has offended us from the verdict of our judgment then we continue our journey with God, seeking to align the desires of our heart with God's heart. Whether the journey of forgiveness is of a short duration or whether it takes years, the journey will be steeped in grace. Inner peace and freedom will emerge as the grace of forgiveness continues to ripen within us. The conditions for reconciliation requires that the offender take responsibility for the offense, desires to be forgiven, and is willing to receive forgiveness. Then in the spirit of reconciliation both the forgiver and the injurer are able to interact with one another in peace and compassion.

❖

In reflecting on the quote and question for each Friday of each of the six weeks of Lent, you are invited to look within the fabric of your life regarding what love calls for in both receiving and bestowing forgiveness and reconciliation.

❖

Surrendering with Trust

Trust does not exist in a vacuum. It is relational.
It binds and intertwines us with the human and the holy,
to creation and all the created and to all our experience with them.

Jean Blomquist[29]

The final act of Jesus' life is an act of surrender, an entrusting of his life and his whole being into the hands of God. The scriptures record his last words this way. "Father, into your hands I commit my spirit."[30] The finality of these words might suggest to some that as an activity within a constellation of interactive movements, this one is reserved for the end. But no, not at all. As we have noted earlier, the work of the Spirit unfolds within us in a fashion that is as unpredictable as a flag unfurling in the wind. Thus, surrendering with trust to God is meant to be an attitude for living as much as of dying, an attitude that is as constant and unfailing as breathing itself. Letting go into God is an ever-present invitation within us. It is like an interior current seeking to draw us deeper into relinquishing control and yielding with steadfast and unwavering trust to our heart's deepest longing for God. When the final act of surrender is called forth from us, we will welcome it with a free, unfettered, yes.

As Jesus yielded in his own life's journey to a deeper interior movement of trust and surrender to God, it becomes a part of his teachings. "Do not let your hearts be troubled. Trust in God still; and trust in me."[31] How do we acquire trust in God? We develop trust on the basis of relationship. Our parents are our first teachers about the meaning of trust. From them we learn also to trust other human beings, and then to grow to trust our own life processes. Each of us establishes definite boundaries, creates certain textures of faith, and develops fine layers of trust within us.

One such layer is that of passive trust. We take a passive unreflective stance for example when we operate a microwave oven assuming it is safe and reliable. Another layer of trust is anticipatory and practical. When we drive a car and approach a green light, we anticipate with trust that cars coming at us from a perpendicular direction will stop on red. There is a layer of trust that is intentional in which we act out of purpose, like following the guidance of a ski instructor down a challenging slope. Then there is the level of trust that takes us into risk and far beyond it, like jumping out the window of a burning building on the basis of a stranger's words, "Don't be afraid. I'll catch you." In moments like this we relinquish total control and leap into the mind and heart of God, "being sure of what we hope for and certain of what we do not see"[32]

❖

On Saturday of each week, you reflect on trust, its layers, its invitations, and its risks. You will reflect on observations from six remarkable people who navigated their life's journey and surrendered with trust in the face of unforeseen challenges and consequences.

❖

A Journey with Six Remarkable Companions

We have chosen five individuals of the twentieth century to accompany our journey through the first five weeks of Lent, and Jesus of Nazareth to befriend the final week of our journey. We chose these individuals because their life's journey and their life-altering decisions changed the course of their lives and in due course influence our own. The life's journey of each of these five individuals is remarkable; together they are extraordinary.

Each Sunday of the six weeks of Lent begins with a biographical sketch of the spiritual companion with whom we will journey during the week. The biographical sketch of each companion represents a collage of snapshots that seeks to give a context to their life's journey as well as a focus on the deep spiritual resolve of their life. After the biographical sketch, there is a personal reflection. It is designed to invite you into your own musing about the person with whom you will journey during the week. It is also meant to open you to a reflection on your life in light of all that is at work in Jesus' willingness to take up his cross, and surrender his life to God's will.

During the first week of Lent, we reflect on the words of Helen Keller's journey. Her life represents the transforming power of a cross, carried with dignity, strength of mind, and a compassionate regard for humankind. Dietrich Bonhoeffer, a martyr who willingly staked his life and died in a concentration camp as the price of discipleship is our companion for the second week of Lent. During the third week, we journey with Simone Weil, a remarkable woman who was an influential philosopher, social activist, mystic, and religious seeker. We are guided throughout the fourth week of Lent by the words of Martin Luther King, Jr. His life and work for social justice, human equality, and peace continue to be an inspiration for all spiritual seekers. During the fifth week of Lent we walk with Mother Teresa of Calcutta, who demonstrated for the whole world the deepest meaning of "love one another just as I have loved you."[33] The final week of Lent, Holy Week, is a week with Jesus, focusing on his fidelity to his resolve to go to Jerusalem and the interior movements that supported both his life-altering decision and its consequences.

How to Use The Journal

This journal is intended to be a way to record personal insights, feelings, or important remembrances that show up during meditation. It can also be a place to note questions or wonderings that come from an enduring moment of reflection. A journal page can be a special place to write down a prayer for oneself, for another, or for a situation in the world. It can also be a wonderful place to create a poem, sketch an image, doodle, or draw a symbol that represents what is occurring in one's reflections.

However the journal is used, it becomes an account of an intentional journey, a journey undertaken with no preconceived ideas of how it should be, where it must go, or necessarily when and how it ought to end. However one chooses to use this journal, it is designed to facilitate the discovery of what is occurring at a deeper, reflective level in the wider domain of one's mind, heart, and spirit.

The quotes for reflection are drawn from either the writings or written sayings of each of the six companions you will journey with each week. The question for reflection following the quote is either an open-ended question or a closed question. In both cases, they are intended to stretch you in considering your relationship with God, other people, and the life around you. They seek to draw you deeper into the various layers of your heart's deepest longings.

JOURNAL AS A DAILY PERSONAL LENTEN PRACTICE

If you use this journal as a daily personal Lenten practice, we have a few suggestions. We first recommend that you begin your practice with a prayer that acknowledges the desires of your heart in this time of being with God. Take a few minutes to enter into silence. Some people are comfortable with closing their eyes as they enter the quiet; others prefer to simply lower their eyes. More important, be conscious of your breathing, slowly drawing in a deep breath and exhaling the breath of life in you just as slowly. Sitting up straight in a chair, and gently relaxing your shoulders with your hands comfortably on your lap, is a physical stance most people find helpful in becoming still. Repeat the conscious breathing in and breathing out several times. If you hear a noise around you, let it be, make nothing of it. If you find thoughts dancing in your mind, do not entertain them; rather allow them to waltz on by.

When you feel your inner self quieting in the silence, read the quote for the day slowly two or three times, each time slower than the last. We recommend you read it at least once out loud. In hearing it you will receive it differently than just entertaining it quietly in your mind. Let the quote's meaning speak to you. Sit with the quote for several minutes. When the time feels right, make any notations you wish in your journal that may have occurred in being with the quote. Then turn to the question, reading it over slowly in the same way as the quote. In the silence ponder the question in light of the quote, paying attention to whatever emerges from your reflection. When the time is ripe, make an appropriate notation in your journal. When your reflection draws to a close, end your time as you began with a prayer that speaks to the deep desire of your heart for God.

JOURNAL AS A GROUP LENTEN PRACTICE

This journal also lends itself to being used in a small group setting, either on a daily basis if one lives in community, or in the setting of a weekly gathering such as a prayer group. We suggest that someone be designated to lead the group into prayer, followed by an entering into silence as described above. After several minutes of silence, the group leader would read the quote two or three times slowly, followed by several minutes of silence. Next, the leader would read the question two or three times slowly, followed by another long period of silence, between ten and twenty minutes. When an appropriate time has occurred, the leader would allow ten to fifteen minutes for making notations in the journal. The next half hour would be given over to group reflective sharing. From out of the silence, individuals who wished to share something from their time with the quote or question could do so. It is not a time of discussion, nor to ask questions, nor to give advice, but rather a time to share with one another the graces of being together in the Spirit.

By faithfully attending to this daily practice without any personal agenda of tying to accomplish something, the Spirit tutors us in our relationship with God and informs our heart as to what changes may be called for in our life's journey.

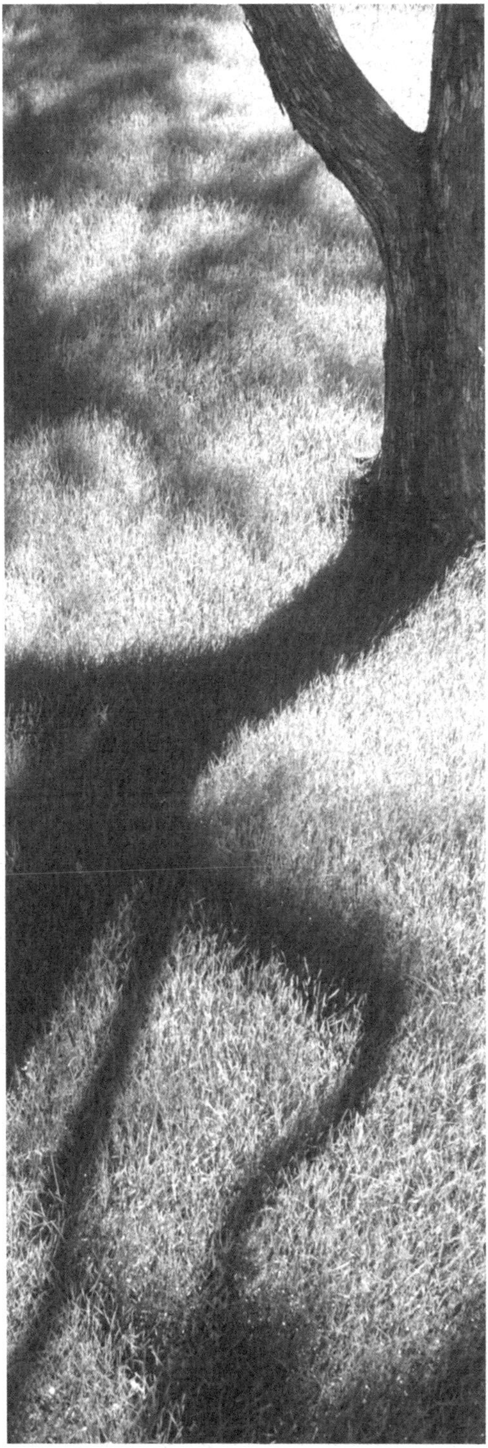

Part Two

Beginning The Journey

The most frightening demons are the spiritual ones that have no names, no faces, and no horns. Never painted red, spiritual demons can beset and besiege the strongest soul.

Anne Marie Drew[34]

Our six weeks of Lent (36 days) are preceded by four days commencing with Ash Wednesday, giving us the total of forty days. The Sundays of Lent are not counted because they are celebrations of the Lord's resurrection. The forty days Jesus spent in the wilderness symbolically recall the Israelites' historical and spiritual journey of forty years wandering in the desert as well as Moses' forty days and forty nights on Mt. Sinai when he received the Ten Commandments.[35]

As we commence with this Lenten journey, we begin on Ash Wednesday, looking back at how God has been watching carefully over our life's journey. Placed in God's providential care, we then consider the nature of Jesus' temptations by the devil. In looking at each of the devil's three enticements, we come into contact with the counter-cultural nature of the spiritual life. In other words, if we center our life in power, wealth, and material possessions to satisfy the deepest longing of our heart, it subverts our attention away from God who alone can fulfill the heart's deepest longings. The lure of these temptations is generally subtle but subversive. Thus, when we intentionally pay attention to how these enticements can undermine our relationship with God, it can be unsettling on the one hand, and provide a way open on the other hand to a life-altering change in the way we live.

So we begin the journey.

Ash Wednesday
1st Day of Lent

The Lord your God has blessed you in all the work of your hands. He has watched over your journey through this vast desert. These forty years the Lord your God has been with you, and you have not lacked anything.
— Deuteronomy 2:7

One of my most enduring experiences when I felt God watching over and guiding me was . . .

Thursday after Ash Wednesday
2nd Day of Lent

The tempter approached and said to him, "If you are the Son of God, command that these stones become loaves of bread. He said in reply, "It is written: 'One does not live by bread alone, but by every word that comes forth from the mouth of God.'" — *Matthew 4:4-3*

What sustains me during times when I find my inner and outer life being tested?

Friday after Ash Wednesday
3rd Day of Lent

Then the devil took him to the holy city, and made him stand on the parapet of the temple, and said to him, "If you are the Son of God, throw yourself down. For it is written: 'He will command his angels concerning you and with their hands they will support you, lest you dash your foot against a stone.'" Jesus answered him, "Again it is written, 'You shall not put the Lord, your God, to the test.'"

Matthew 4:6-7

When I want to take the easy way out from the challenges of my life's journey, where do I turn for strength and courage to stand up to being tested?

Saturday after Ash Wednesday
4th Day of Lent

Then he took him up and showed him all the kingdoms of the world in a single instant. The devil said to him, "I shall give to you all this power and their glory; for it has been handed over to me, and I may give it to whomever I wish. All this will be yours, if you worship me." Jesus said to him in reply, "It is written: 'You shall worship the Lord, your God, and him alone shall you serve.'" — Luke 4:5-8

When I find I am being lured by desires for material things and by the worldly realities of secularism, I . . .

First Sunday of Lent

A Week with Helen Keller

(1880-1968)

Helen Keller, daughter of an editor and his wife, was born in Tuscumbia, Alabama, in 1880, with normal hearing and sight, both of which were lost during a sudden fever when she was nineteen months old. Known to many as the uncontrollable child in the movie, *The Miracle Worker*, who learns to communicate through the patience and skill of her teacher, Annie Sullivan, Helen Keller is a symbol of a remarkable woman who overcame disabling blindness and deafness.

Frustrated by an inability to understand others and to share her desires and ideas, Helen acted out her anger. When her parents realized she needed special assistance, they sought the advice of Alexander Graham Bell who had developed a visual communication system for the deaf. Bell suggested they hire a graduate of the Perkins Institute for the Blind. Annie Sullivan came to live in the Keller home and became Helen's teacher and companion until Sullivan's death.

Annie taught Helen to communicate using the manual alphabet in Helen's hand, teaching lip-reading by touch and reading with Braille. This enabled Helen to gain an education. As a teenager, Helen attended the Wright-Humanson School for the Deaf and the Cambridge School for Young Ladies before enrolling in Radcliff University. Helen graduated with honors in 1904 from Radcliff.

From the early days as a toddler, through her college years at a prestigious university, Helen struggled to learn the complexities and nuances of communication. A bright and curious child, Helen persevered in laborious instruction and isolation. Annie Sullivan taught her to be an independent woman.

Well aware of the benefits of her life and the complexities of world issues, Helen became an advocate for services for the disabled, particularly the deaf and blind. It is not clear when she made the decisions to advocate for advances she had received due to privilege and persistence. Perhaps the turning points in her life were continual and not dramatic but were nonetheless significant decisions that created models for others to follow. Her campaigns and speeches influenced thinking in her time and continue to inspire leaders today.

Helen read continuously and developed strong opinions also about the economic and political climate of her times. Helen became a socialist and an advocate for women's suffrage and birth control. She spoke out against the First World War and warned about the proliferation of weapons.

Visiting Hiroshima and Nagasaki three years after the dropping of the nuclear bomb, Helen advocated for an end to war. She visited many soldiers in hospitals. She traveled to many countries and earned the respect of many famous individuals including the President of the United States. Impulsive and outspoken, she did not hesitate to let her views be known. She wrote letters, made personal contacts and traveled worldwide to seek equality for all. She championed equal rights for African Americans and decried child labor. Later in life, she became a primary fundraiser and spokesperson for the American Federation for the Blind.

Fascinated with her intelligence and the story related to her disability, others made Helen the source of Hollywood movies and of books, most of which portrayed her childhood and the miracles of her performance against daunting odds. She became entrapped in this image and rebelled against the "plaster saint" portrayal. Time and time again, she needed to let her true self come forth when the overwhelming pressure to submit to a sanitized image was compelling. To stay afloat financially, she and Annie Sullivan spent years traveling in a vaudeville show in a 20-minute sketch of how she learned to talk. She wrote a number of books and essays, which were published in an attempt to have the world know her thoughts and ideas beyond the blindness and deafness.

When Annie Sullivan died, Helen faced a crisis, trying to make an adjustment to a life without her teacher and lifelong companion. Helen had become part of the Macy family when Annie married so the death of this constant person was a pivotal time. While she was independent, Helen could not live alone. Others took the place of Annie but all had images of Helen that they tried to force upon her.

Helen's ashes were placed in the St. Joseph of Arimathea Chapel in the Washington Cathedral in Washington, D.C., near the ashes of Annie Sullivan after her death in 1968. Despite her wishes to have a Swedenborgian funeral, Swedenborgian being the religion she preferred, her family arranged for a Presbyterian service, continuing their attempts to shape Helen into who they wanted her to be.

A PERSONAL REFLECTION ❖ HELEN KELLER

The more I delved into the life of Helen Keller, the more I found her life inspiring, and yet at other times she seemed to be an enigma. Many times I would just sit quietly imaginatively wandering through this or that anecdote of her life's story. So many questions would emerge. So many wonderings would lure me into lingering with the intangible and the spiritual dimensions that encircled her life. How did this intelligent woman, when pushed into an interior world with the sudden onset of lost sight and hearing, find the inner call and strength to step out into a world that did not welcome or understand her disabling condition? What inner struggles raged between her desperate desire to be independent and actively engaged when the limitations of her training and disabilities forced her into dependence?

Helen is a woman of incomparable resolve whose inner resourcefulness enabled her to shape her world in spite of the way a disability often shaped others of her time. While relentlessly constrained, she was unrestrained in her advocacy for the poor and the disabled. A champion for the case for peace rather than war, she willingly took on Presidents and world leaders. What in her spirit caused her to challenge external limits? How did she deal with the darkness of loss? Was she angry with God when she struggled to accept the external limitations that were not of her choosing?

As I walk this Lenten journey with Helen Keller, I find myself roaming around in my own prayer, sitting with the questions that must have nagged at her as they do me. How did she discern God's purpose for her life? What forgiveness and reconciliation issues were confronting her? As she takes up her cross and dies to what the world and perhaps what she expected of herself, what emerges? Is it the child that God loves? What speaks to me of this life as lived by Helen? How does her journey challenge or encourage me? What does it say to me about my life in God?

Monday ❖ 5th Day of Lent
"Discerning God's Purpose"

Many persons have a wrong idea of what constitutes true happiness. It is not attained through self-gratification but through fidelity to a worthy purpose. — *Helen Keller*

What do I understand to be God's "worthy purpose" for me and how do I exhibit faithfulness in wanting to fulfill it?

Tuesday ❖ 6th Day of Lent
"Losing Life to Find It"

One can never consent to creep when one feels an impulse to soar.

Helen Keller

As I continue my life's journey, what inspires me to want to lose my life for God's sake in order to find it?

Wednesday ❖ 7th Day of Lent
"Taking Up Your Cross"

Although the world is full of suffering, it is full also of the overcoming of it.
— Helen Keller

Who inspires me by overcoming suffering? How might this inspiration influence the way I carry my cross?

Thursday ❖ 8th Day of Lent
"Dying and Rising"

Only through experience of trial and suffering can the soul be strengthened, ambition inspired, and success achieved.

Helen Keller

What trials and sufferings have served to prune me so my life might be strengthened to yield more fruit?

Friday ❖ 9th Day of Lent
"Forgiving and Reconciling"

The best and most beautiful things in the world cannot be seen or even touched. They must be felt within the heart. — *Helen Keller*

One of the most freeing experiences of my life was when I forgave myself for . . .

Saturday ❖ 10th Day of Lent
"Surrendering with Trust"

When one door of happiness closes, another opens; but often we look so long at the closed door that we do not see the one which has been opened for us.
— Helen Keller

What door(s) is opening before me that calls me to trust, to open it, and to walk through it freely?

Second Sunday of Lent

A Week with Dietrich Bonhoeffer

(1906-1945)

Born to a prominent professor of neurology and psychiatry, Dietrich Bonhoeffer grew up in a large family with access to relatives and scholars of renown. While his Lutheran family was not active in their congregation, Bonhoeffer descended from a theologian grandfather and a church historian great grandfather. Not particularly religious as a child, Bonhoeffer surprised his parents when he decided to study theology, an academic more than a church pursuit at that time in Germany. Receiving his doctorate at age 21, he worked for a year in Barcelona, Spain as a pastor.

Soon after Hitler was elected as Chancellor of Germany in 1933, Bonhoeffer began to speak out on the German radio about the idolatry of pledging allegiance to the Fuhrer. Hitler was systematically assuming control of the state controlled Lutheran church and Bonhoeffer was one of the first to recognize the underlying evil beneath the externally seductive benefits of employments, vacations, and a Volkswagen car. Suspicious of the racial purity laws, Bonhoeffer encouraged his brother-in-law, who was Jewish, to leave the country. With friends, Dietrich helped craft a confession statement declaring Jesus as the one Lord, a statement not endorsed by the State Lutheran church, which remained silent about the active integration of government into the church. Soon afterward, when Hitler sent storm troopers to the church, Bonhoeffer publicly confronted them. From this time on he was sanctioned about making public pronouncements.

As leader of a clandestine seminary in Pomerania, Bonhoeffer trained pastors for an anti-Nazi Lutheran church. He emphasized the issues of discipleship and community recognizing the pastors would need to support one another as the members of the early Christian church had done. He introduced the practice of monastic silence in the seminary. The content of his lectures are featured in his books, *The Cost of Discipleship* and *Life Together*. The Gestapo disbanded the seminary in 1940 and the seminarians were sent to the front as soldiers.

Dietrich went to the United States in 1939, at the encouragement of his friends, to study at Union Seminary in New York. It was here that he became impressed with the black religious leaders in Harlem and began to ask the question of what it means to be a Christian. These relationships ignited a desire to be involved in ecumenical dialogue and to study the issues of Christianity as it is revealed in doctrine and in ordinary life. Bonhoeffer expressed concern that many of the Christian churches in America lacked commitment to the gospel teachings he found so prominently proclaimed in the Black churches.

Friends encouraged him to remain when the war began, knowing that he was a marked man if he returned to Germany. However, Bonhoeffer felt a call to return to his homeland so he could one day be part of the reconstruction. He sensed a call from God to walk into struggle and thus returned to Germany only six weeks after his arrival in the United States, stating in a letter to Richard Niebuhr, "I shall have no right to participate in the reconstruction of Christian life in Germany after the war if I do not share the trials of this time with my people…" [36]

Struggling with ethical issues of the spirit of the commandments against the overwhelming evil of the national leadership, Bonhoeffer decided to join relatives and friends who were part of the resistance movement. Over time, he became an official spy for the Nazi party, a cover for his actual covert operations. As the awareness of the extermination of the Jews was more and more obvious, Bonhoeffer and other military intelligence officers plotted a way to assassinate Hitler. When the plot named Operation 7 failed, he and the others were rounded up and sent to prison. His first imprisonment at Tegel was somewhat less restrictive than later ones would be as he was allowed supervised visits from his fiancée Maria von Wedemeyer who brought him books and letters. Over time, he was moved to other prisons and finally to Flossenburg where he was hanged days before Hitler committed suicide.

While in prison, Bonhoeffer remained a pastor to his fellow inmates. He helped keep calm and order as prisoners heard the air raids and the apparent shootings of their number. Guards were impressed by his obvious calm and service and smuggled out many of his writings, known today as *Letters and Papers from Prison*. Six months after the war, Maria went from camp to camp searching for Dietrich, finally learning of his death. While Dietrich's remains were never located, his championing for Christians to be active in the political and public life continues. He lived intimately in the struggles of the oppressed, the despised, the hunted, and the suffering, recognizing that God had called him to a deep and risky walk, but a walk where the Spirit accompanied him. A prison doctor who witnessed Bonhoeffer said, "Through the half-opened door, I saw Pastor Bonhoeffer still in his prison clothes, kneeling in fervent prayer to the Lord his God. The devotion and evident conviction of being heard that I saw in the prayer of this intensively captivating man moved me to the depths."[37]

A PERSONAL REFLECTION ❖ DIETRICH BONHOEFFER

I have always admired Dietrich Bonhoeffer. His books, *Letters and Papers from Prison* and *The Cost of Discipleship*, have long inspired me. His life and his death captivate me. He challenges me at a level few other people do. I admire the clarity and strength of his bold and daring decision to return to Germany and take on Adolf Hitler. At the same time, I struggle with his decision to participate in a plot to assassinate Hitler as it stands in such stark contrast to the stance Jesus took in his encounter with evil.

The journey of Dietrich Bonhoeffer from pulpit to prison to martyr invites me into many questions, most poignantly, how my faith and sense of a call might lead me into places I dare not go. His ponderings and deep anguishing cries of "Who am I?" strike at my own wonderings of whether I am who God calls me to be. I delight with his conclusion that despite my weakness, God, I am thine.

Whenever I sit with recollections of his life or his writings, I find myself grappling with so many of the systemic injustices in the world, and my own feelings of powerlessness to respond to them. Do I trust that with God's help I can become a maker of peace and a doer of justice?

Knowing the cross he was taking up, realizing the risks of literally losing his life, I am drawn to the deep quality of his trust that God was at work at this horrible and dark time in the world. I wonder what advocacy might I be called to. I also ask myself if the real cross was not the plot against Hitler as it was the call to be faithful and forgiving while in prison.

Monday ❖ 11th Day of Lent
"Discerning God's Purpose"

Who am I? They mock me, these lonely questions of mine. Whoever I am, thou knowest, O God, I am thine. — *Dietrich Bonhoeffer*

What is my deepest desire for God and how does this fit with my understanding of who I am?

Tuesday ❖ 12th Day of Lent
"Losing Life to Find It"

O Lord God, great distress has come upon me. My cares threaten to crush me, And I do not know what to do. — Dietrich Bonhoeffer

---

What concerns, dependencies, and attachments get in the way of the life I must claim in my journey with God?

Wednesday ❖ 13th Day of Lent
"Taking Up Your Cross"

To endure the cross is not tragedy; it is the suffering which is the fruit of an exclusive allegiance to Jesus Christ. — *Dietrich Bonhoeffer*

The cross Jesus carried brought him into solidarity with all humankind. With whom do I experience solidarity in the cross I carry or help others to carry?

Thursday ❖ 14th Day of Lent
"Dying and Rising"

The cross is laid on every Christian. It begins with the call to abandon the attachments of this world. It is that dying of the old man which is the result of his encounter with Christ. — Dietrich Bonhoeffer

What attachments need to die in me so I am free to encounter Christ?

Friday ❖ 15th Day of Lent
"Forgiving and Reconciling"

The service of forgiveness is rendered by one to the others daily. It occurs, without words, in the intercessions for one another.

Dietrich Bonhoeffer

If I were to forgive others today, for whom would I intercede, and why?

Saturday ❖ 16th Day of Lent
"Surrendering with Trust"

Faint not nor fear, but go out to the storm and the action, trusting in God whose commandment you faithfully follow.

Dietrich Bonhoeffer

In the world in which I live my life, what storm(s) calls me to yield wholly and entirely to trust in God?

Third Sunday of Lent

A Week with Simone Weil

(1909-1943)

Patriot, mystic, activist, intellectual and secular Jew, Simone Weil believed in the redemptive power of manual labor, devoting her life to teaching, labor unions, and work among the common man. Having several religious experiences, Simone became a worshipping Roman Catholic who refused baptism and raised questions about the institutional church. Dying at an early age of 34 from anorexia, Simone journeyed from a pampered childhood to years of labor meetings, hunger, illness, and fascination with the rituals of the church.

Born into an intellectual family in Paris, Simone, a bright and thoughtful child, felt overshadowed by her genius brother. Recognized for her own intellectual prowess, Weil became a teacher when the European economy followed the U.S. Depression. Aware of the economic plight of many around her, Simone began to teach political activism to the labor unions. An admirer of Marx, she first advocated for Socialist policies, only to become disenchanted when she saw how the socialist governments actually performed. She wrote articles for left wing militant publications and worked in a factory to understand first hand the plight of the working class. Weil later moved to Barcelona where she volunteered for the front. Soon injured and weak, she returned to France and teaching. Her migraine headaches, eating disorder and other ailments would continue to plague her. She continued to write about the oppression of factory piecework, the treatment of women, and the redemptive aspect of suffering. Simone believed suffering was the root to spirituality so she remained close to the poor in an attempt to identify with them.

Visiting Assisi, she fell in love with the Mass in the Chapel of Santa Maria degli Angeli. This was her second life-altering religious experience, having had a similar experience years earlier while viewing the sights of a Portuguese fishing village. In 1938, she visited Solesmus, a Benedictine monastery where she claims she felt the passion of Christ and became enamored with the sacraments. In Simone's quest for spiritual growth, she began a study of comparative religions and the life of St. Francis of Assisi. Finding the Mass appealing, she continued to write also about the authority of the Roman church. Simone refused to be baptized but bathed herself in the liturgy and the hymns.

Weil's beliefs were influenced by Eastern religious thought. She felt the world need to be governed by laws because humans, she believed were indifferent. She believed that as we continue to painfully accept God's absence, we come to know God's presence. Seeing the implicit love of God in compassion for a neighbor, in rituals, especially prayer, and in love for the order and beauty of the world, Simone advocated that beauty is good by itself. She felt an affinity to Job, because of her own suffering of mind and body. She proposed that we wait passively for God to give us God's gifts rather than trying to seek them.

Some of her published works include *Waiting for God, Gravity and Grace,* and *The Need for Roots*.

A PERSONAL REFLECTION ❖ SIMONE WEIL

When I linger with Simone Weil's life story, I feel dazzled and mystical and passionate at the same time. She confuses, inspires, and intrigues me. Her daring authenticity sometime gets in my way of truly appreciating and understanding her. I am puzzled and lured by the quotes that are representative of her life. She seems so driven by her deep passions for justice, all the while lured into a mysterious relationship with God. Her willingness to give up the self others imposed on her in order to be authentic with her inner desires is a striking image.

I imagine a rich but complex woman, who feels diminished by being compared to her brother; who puts into play the ultimate power move against her dominating parents; and who suffers isolation by a restrictive culture that could not appreciate her insights and her gifted intellect. The positions she took and the decisions she made often took her to places most people would not go. I can understand her desire to step into the grime and hard life of the factory to experience first hand the life of the laborer, but, I don't understand why she lingered there so long. Was her sense of justice such a deep call that she would surrender her own well being to be anything less than completely authentic? I am so quick to judge her when I discover she became ill and allowed the illness to ultimately impair her life. But isn't that what mystics have done over the years? Is this the cost of embracing the cross for the sake of love?

The mystical encounters that lead to her dedication to the Roman Catholic Mass, I also find intriguing. To see how liturgical ritual spoke to her heart and to image her trusting in a mystery she could not get her arms around sustains my desire for the same, resting in prayer and compassion. I admire the feistiness that allows her to maintain her integrity in her stands against some church practices, her willingness to embrace the truths of Eastern religion and her unabashed candor in her writings. As I walk with her this week, I ponder the qualities of my own surrendering and trust.

Monday ❖ 17th Day of Lent
"Discerning God's Purpose"

To be a hero or a heroine, one must give an order to oneself.

Simone Weil

In my journey with God,
what do I resolve to do to renew my life?

Tuesday ❖ 18th Day of Lent
"Losing Life to Find It"

To be rooted is perhaps the most important and least recognized need of the human soul. — *Simone Weil*

In order for my life to become centered and rooted in God, I . . .

Wednesday ❖ 19th Day of Lent
"Taking Up Your Cross"

The love of our neighbor in all its fullness simply means being able to say to him, "What are you going through?" — *Simone Weil*

The need of the person in need makes a claim on everyone who recognizes the need. When I look upon the cross that another person carries and ponder what that person is going through, what is love's claim on me?

Thursday ❖ 20th Day of Lent
"Dying and Rising"

Every time that I think of the crucifixion of Christ, I commit the sin of envy.
— Simone Weil

What sin cries out from within me that longs for the healing and redemptive power of the crucifixion of Christ?

Friday ❖ 21st Day of Lent
"Forgiving and Reconciling"

Human beings are so made that the ones who do the crushing feel nothing; it is the person crushed who feels what is happening. Unless one has placed oneself on the side of the oppressed, to feel with them, one cannot understand. — *Simone Weil*

When have I felt the weight of being crushed and emptied out by a form of oppression? What did it call forth from me regarding forgiveness?

Saturday ❖ 22nd Day of Lent
"Surrendering with Trust"

Two prisoners whose cells adjoin communicate with each other by knocking on the wall. The wall is the thing which separates them but is also their means of communication. It is the same with us and God. Every separation is a link. — *Simone Weil*

What separates me from God? For me to trust that this very separation could be a link to God, I . . .

Fourth Sunday of Lent

A Week with Martin Luther King, Jr.

(1929-1968)

Martin Luther King, Jr., recognized by a national holiday, is the premier model of the Civil Rights advocate, particularly during the 1950s and 1960s. An ordained Baptist minister with a doctorate in systematic theology, King practiced the tenets of his Christian beliefs and the practices of Gandhi's non-violent stance to lead organizations to challenge the racial oppression accepted by most within the United States.

Martin Luther King, Jr., was pastor of the Ebenezer Baptist Church in Atlanta, a congregation his father had served and the place where he is buried. As a student of Christian theology, with an emphasis on the relationship of faith to the lives of oppressed people, King began the seeds of advocacy that would influence his ministry. King was influenced by Gandhi's work and writings, the sermons of white Protestant ministers who spoke out against racism and Benjamin Mays, the president of Morehouse College. King recognized a call to serve humanity.

Serving as minister of Dexter Avenue Baptist Church, King became active in the larger community. In his farewell letter to the congregation, he writes, "Unknowingly and unexpectedly, I was catapulted into the leadership of the Montgomery Movement."[38] As president of the Montgomery Improvement Association, King and others organized a bus protest that lasted a year. He persisted with the organization to file a lawsuit that eventually led to an injunction against segregated seating practices, despite a bombing of his home. This case went to the Supreme Court and became a new way to integrate public life. King writes in his autobiography as he leaves Montgomery, "It was not easy to decide to leave a city where Negroes resisted injustice magnificently and followed a method of nonviolent struggle that became one of the glowing epics of the twentieth century. I hated to leave Montgomery but the people realized that the call from the whole South was one that could not be denied."[39]

In 1957, King helped found the Southern Christian Leadership Conference, SCLC, which became a life-altering event in his life. This group led numerous protests and marches to protest racist practices in public places. Arrested in Birmingham, he penned a letter to other clergy reminding them of the moral imperative for justice. His keynote address at the Washington March in 1963, "I Have A Dream," added to the political momentum of the Civil Rights movement. Later marches led to the Voting Rights Act of 1965. King opposed the war in Vietnam and began to shift his focus to economic disparities in the North.

King's journey was risky and eventually led to his assassination in 1968. He was threatened and assaulted by blacks and whites. Not all understand or supported his insistence for non-violence. Some in the Black Power movement resented the media attention given to him. Others felt overwhelmed by the social changes that seemed to be rapidly changing the public landscape.

Martin Luther King, Jr., often told stories of blacks who lived out their lives from a source of faith in God. Calling himself a drum major for righteousness, King believed love is a durable power strong enough to make sweeping changes. In 1964, King was awarded the Noble Prize for Peace. He understood the role of a prophet and recognized the global implications for justice for African Americans.

A PERSONAL REFLECTION ❖ MARTIN LUTHER KING, JR.

Pictures of Martin Luther King, Jr., are so fresh in my mind, it is as though the ink has not yet dried. These images haunt me, as does his stance of non-violence. I saw him first as a man, then as a father, and finally as a pastor. It was the stature of his humanity that seized me most of all, much more than his prominence as a national hero. As I step quietly into his shoes and wander around in some of the notable events of his life, I see him arguing with God and pleading for mercy. I imagine him in long conversations with God, and God giving birth to the clarity of his words, and the focus of his prophetic vision much like the prophets of old. His words still cut like a sharp laser right to my heart and keep me aware of hatred and hatred's ugly renderings of injustice. When I sit with his words, I wonder how he experienced God leading him, how he lived through dark moments of struggle, inner doubts, and where he found God in the dark?

I sometimes get lost in my culture's expectations and workings. I feel deeply for the people who struggle with systemic inequality, discrimination, and injustice. Their needs make a claim on me. Would I be willing to take a bold, non-violent stand that would put me in jail or set up my family for potential threats? And despite my meager efforts at advocacy, I find I am often guilty of the appalling silence that King notes. I have not marched. I have not lived as a minority. I have not experienced racial oppression.

Martin Luther King, Jr.'s, life, his journey with God, and his willingness to take up a cross that led to his death is both a model and a disturbing image for me. It leaves me with a personal and collective question—what does God demand of us in behalf of God's children?

Monday ❖ 23rd Day of Lent
"Discerning God's Purpose"

I just want to do God's will. And he's allowed me to go to the mountain.
Martin Luther King, Jr.

For me to want to do God's will with all of my heart, with no strings attached, I . . .

Tuesday ❖ 24th Day of Lent
"Losing Life to Find It"

I submit to you that if a man hasn't discovered something he will die for, he isn't fit to live. — *Martin Luther King, Jr.*

On what am I willing to stake my life, that is, willing to lose it, in order to find it for the love of God?

Wednesday ❖ 25th Day of Lent
"Taking Up Your Cross"

The ultimate measure of a man is not where he stands in moments of comfort, but where he stands at times of challenge and controversy.

Martin Luther King, Jr.

What cross do I see in my life or the life around me that is a source of challenge or controversy for me? What stand does it call for me to take?

Thursday ❖ 26th Day of Lent
"Dying and Rising"

Hatred paralyzes life; love releases it. Hatred confuses life; love harmonizes it. Hatred darkens life; love illumines it.

Martin Luther King, Jr.

In my heart, what form or manifestation of hatred would die if I exposed my heart to the unifying, freeing, enlightening energy of love?

Friday ❖ 27th Day of Lent
"Forgiving and Reconciling"

We will all have to repent in this generation not merely for the hateful words and actions of the bad people but for the appalling silence of the good people. — *Martin Luther King, Jr.*

For which acts of inexcusable silence in my life am I now called to repent?

Saturday ❖ 28th Day of Lent
"Surrendering with Trust"

I believe that unarmed truth and unconditional love will have the final word in reality. That is why right, temporarily defeated, is stronger than evil triumphant. — *Martin Luther King, Jr.*

The most daring challenge I experience for truth and unconditional love in my life is . . .

Fifth Sunday of Lent

A Week with Mother Teresa

(1910-1997)

In the 1920s, an Albanian teenager named Agnes Bojaxhiu went to her local priest, Father Franjco Jambrekovich to inform him she desired to be a missionary. Advised by him to pray about this call, Agnes reluctantly agreed to wait. Then, in May of 1931, after a two-year novitiate of training and formation, Agnes took the vows of poverty, chastity, and obedience as a Sister of Loreto in India and assumed the name of Teresa after Saint Therese of Lisieux. Her first assignment was to be a teacher in a parochial school for middle class girls in Calcutta. Teresa taught geography and history at St. Mary's school and soon became the headmistress. In the 1940s as Mahatma Gandhi rose as a moral leader to free India from 500 years of British rule, Teresa talked about the political issues in classes and took students to visit the poor in the parish. Seeing the poverty of Calcutta, Teresa, on a long, slow and arduous, train trip from Calcutta to Darjeeling, sensed that God was calling her to something else. After two years of prayers, retreats, and spiritual direction, she contacted her Superior General and later the Pope asking permission to be relieved of her position as principal of the school and to leave the Sisters of Loreto so she could work among the poor. This life-altering decision began forming the role and image the world came to know as Mother Teresa.

On August 16, 1948, with a small suitcase and 5 rupees (all of which she gave away), the thirty-eight year old Teresa set out for her new life. She went first for nursing training and then returned to Calcutta to live with a Muslim family who gave her a room rent-free. Their daughter, Subashini Das, joined Teresa in the slums, and together they became the Missionaries of Charity, an organization that over time would have centers throughout the world. The first building, named Nirmal Hriday, home of the pure heart, is where Mother Teresa continued to live. The community grew as many former students joined Teresa in her work. Assuming the leadership of the organization, Mother Teresa became the dominant figure of the Missionaries of Charity.

Mother Teresa began to venture outside of India in the 1960s speaking to groups about her work. In the 1970s she became internationally renown, due in part to the work of Malcolm Muggeridge who highlighted her in his BBC show and his book, *Something Beautiful for God*. Mother received the Nobel Peace Prize in 1979 and went on to visit and be visited by heads of state and noted celebrities.

Sickly as a child, Mother Teresa suffered health problems in her forties and into her seventies and eighties. She underwent several surgeries for her heart in her later years and finally passed to a new life in September of 1997.

A staunch advocate for the poor, Mother Teresa advocated that the poor needed love more than food or shelter. However, over the years, those worldly needs were provided with donations from around the world led by efforts of people like Ann Blaikie who helped with fundraising. Mother herself continued to live in poverty.

Only five feet tall, Mother Teresa was known for her compassion, her vitality, her strong belief in God, and her strength of conviction. She was also known to be a strong willed, determined and fearless leader who stayed tough under pressure and criticism. An opponent of abortion and an obedient servant to the Pope, Mother Teresa was criticized for her adherence to authority and to her inattentiveness to the systemic causes of poverty. She remained faithful to her conviction that life is prayer, that God is present in all of humanity and that her mission was to love the poor where she saw Jesus in all of his distressing disguises. On October 19, 2003, she was beatified by the Pope, a first step toward being canonized a saint.

A PERSONAL REFLECTION ❖ MOTHER TERESA

If I had to choose one word to sum up Mother Teresa, I would select the word, simplicity. When I hold her life up to the light, it is simplicity that weaves together the horizontal and vertical threads of her life into a magnificent tapestry of self-sacrificing love. To most of the world, this self-effacing woman embodies an uncommon surrender to God. She is someone I would like to emulate.

As I sit with her story this week, I admire her humanity and the ever-deepening quality of her trusting relationship with God. When I began reading her life's story, it was like backing into it. Her world-renown work and prominence on the world stage cast a shadow over her very humble beginnings. I was relieved to know that it took a number of years, a season of prayer, a series of meetings with spiritual directors, and finally a stint as a regular teacher and administrator before she stepped into a life of unrelenting poverty and became a role model of lived simplicity. There is a sense of relief in that even a saint didn't get it right, right away.

While I know I am not called to live out my life in the realities of poverty as Mother Teresa did, I find that her friendship with poverty puts flesh on the poverty of spirit I am called to live. I find too, that her simple yet strong statements about the power of love stir me, shifting the concerns of my heart for the plight of the world's poor. Is it that simple? If I rest into that love each day, will it emanate from me, if only in a small way? If I open my heart with deep trust to the divine presence that always embraces me, will I soften my actions to be ones of compassion? Knowing that the Lenten journey of Jesus is the backdrop to all of our lives, I am touched by the admonition of Mother Teresa to forgive just as Jesus modeled that forgiveness for me.

Like all of us in the face of life's heartbreaking incongruities and incredible suffering, I suspect that when Mother Teresa was alone in prayer with God, she prayed as we often do, with tears, with hard questions, and sometimes shaking our fists at God. I can also imagine her with sloped shoulders, holding the dying in her arms, and knowing with deep acceptance that in caring for those in need, she was tending to no one other than God. And I hear within me a quiet deep sigh of trust that God is ever present in the world in the manifestation of self-sacrificing love.

Monday ❖ 29th Day of Lent
"Discerning God's Purpose"

Give yourself fully to God. He will use you to accomplish great things on the condition that you believe much more in His love than in your own weakness.
— Mother Teresa

In order for God to work in and through me to bring about good, I . . .

Tuesday ❖ 30th Day of Lent
"Losing Life to Find It"

The more you have, the more you are occupied, the less you give. But the less you have, the more free you are. — *Mother Teresa*

To truly be responsibly free in my life, what am I willing to lose or reverse in my life?

Wednesday ❖ 31st Day of Lent
"Taking Up Your Cross"

Suffering is nothing by itself. But suffering shared with the passion of Christ is a wonderful gift, the most beautiful gift, a token of love.

Mother Teresa

In what way(s) do I see and experience the cross I carry or the cross others carry as a gift of love?

Thursday ❖ 32nd Day of Lent
"Dying and Rising"

Love, To Be Real, Must Cost—It Must Hurt—It Must Empty Us Of Self.
Mother Teresa

The cost and hurt of love that most empties me of my being centered in myself is . . .

Friday ❖ 33rd Day of Lent
"Forgiving and Reconciling"

If we really want to love we must learn how to forgive.

Mother Teresa

What have I leaned from my experience of being loved that helps me forgive?

Saturday ❖ 34th Day of Lent
"Surrendering with Trust"

Prayer is not asking. Prayer is putting oneself in the hands of God, at his disposition and listening to his voice in the depths of our heart.

Mother Teresa

If I were to entrust my life to God's own prayer for me, I would want to hear God say . . .

A Week with *Jesus of Nazareth*

(C. 4 C.E. -29 C.E.)

Countless books have been written about Jesus of Nazareth, the One known to Christians as the Christ, the Son of God, the Anointed One, the Comforter, the Redeemer, the Savior, the Messiah, the Good Shepherd and the Son of Man. Who was this man about whom so much is written yet for whom there is a scarcity of biographical and historical data?

The significant events of Holy Week that culminate in the passion, death and resurrection of the Christ are the centerpiece of The Story that brings all other events of his life into focus. Having walked the countryside for three years following his baptism by John the Baptist, Jesus preached the messages of love, forgiveness, and the kingdom of God. Now, in this final week that starts with a joyous entry into the city of Jerusalem and then leads to a last supper with his disciples before being led away to imprisonment and crucifixion, Jesus lives out the teachings he has been explaining as he met with crowds and sat with friends. Walking through the streets of Jerusalem after being sentenced by Pontius Pilate, Jesus drags the cross on which he will die. Executed as an insurrectionist on a hill outside the city, he cries out to God to forgive all those who have worked to kill him. Surrendering his spirit to his Father with his last breath, Jesus dies. A few days later, Mary Magdalene encounters him walking the garden, as she grasps that he has risen from the dead. The joyous news of his resurrection becomes the message she runs to tell others and the story that rings out today as the central recollection of all that Jesus represents. The old laws and old ways have been changed and the new law of love is in place.

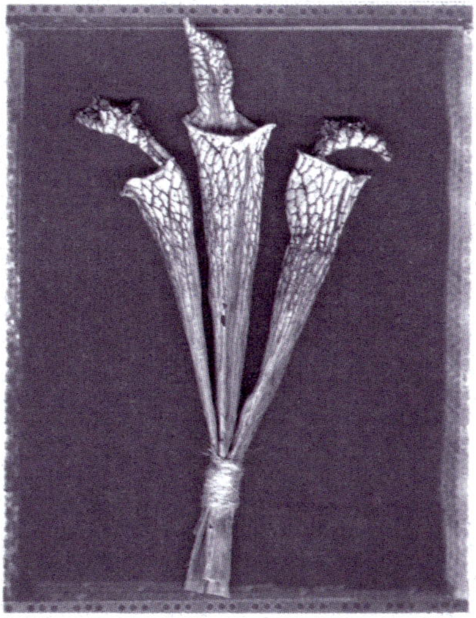

Christians know about Jesus from four narrative gospels. Through the lens of faith and prophecies of the Hebrew Scriptures, these gospel versions tell of his birth in Bethlehem, a period of being tested in the desert and a collection of his teachings as he walked the roads and visited towns and villages. Teaching in parables, he announces a reign of God's love, justice, and peace. His message confuses some, disturbs others, and lures many to leave everything and follow him. Jesus' stories emphasize the need for his followers to love one another, to live together in harmony, to always forgive, and to share what they own. He settles for many the issues of sin and suffering and invites his followers into a new kingdom, a kingdom not of this world but within the heart of each follower.

Primary sources for the life of Jesus come from the four Gospels, and from Letters written to early Christian communities. A few historical sources such as Tacitus, Suetonis, and the Jewish Talmud mention Jesus yet give little historical fact.

A PERSONAL REFLECTION ❖ JESUS OF NAZARETH

I know the Holy Week story of Jesus of Nazareth well. I have heard it read many times over the years and I once walked the path of the Via Dialorosa in Israel. Each time the story seems familiar yet strange. At one level, the story makes sense to me in light of the historical, political, social, and religious milieu in which it unfolds.

I can understand the expediency of his death sentence. Because of the roots of my faith tradition, I understand too his story as it relates to The Story of which we are all a part. As I walk my Lenten journey this week, I am drawn to Jesus' humanity, a human being, I believe, like me in all things but sin. And then I am caught up in a moment in which it makes no sense. Various circumstances, people, and events all converge against him. The plug seems to be pulled on his proclamation of the reign of God. Where is God in this seeming non-sense?

As I reflect on the stories of Jesus' last days, I wish I could yield so freely and without reservation as he did to what unconditional trust always calls for. With my assortment of expectations, beliefs, and conditionings ever before me, I sometimes cringe at a God who demands so much. I seem so unwilling to take any position that requires I totally lose myself. Here are moments when his surrender, his trust, and his ultimate letting go trembles within me much like the earth shook on Good Friday. There are other moments in which I lean into the desire to be free, really free; freed from a self who is bound with trappings of my world and my religion; and freed for his promise of new life.

Monday ❖ 35th Day of Lent
"Discerning God's Purpose"

He went away a second time and prayed, "My Father, if it is not possible for this cup to be taken away unless I drink it, may your will be done." — *Matthew 26:42*

What are the implications for me to claim my understanding of God's purpose for my life?

Tuesday ❖ 36th Day of Lent
"Losing Life to Find It"

Whoever finds his life will lose it, and whoever loses his life for my sake will find it.
— Matthew 10:39

To live life centered in God, what do I need to change in the way I live?

Wednesday ❖ 37th Day of Lent
"Taking Up Your Cross"

He summoned the crowd with his disciples and said to them, "Whoever wishes to come after me must deny himself, take up his cross, and follow me."
— Mark 8:34

How has taking up my cross or sharing in carrying the cross of another, changed my motivation on how I live my life?

Thursday ❖ 38th of Lent
"Dying and Rising"

Amen, amen, I say to you, unless a grain of wheat falls to the ground and dies, it remains just a grain of wheat; but if it dies, it produces much fruit. — *John 12:24*

The experience of letting go that I have come to value most in my life is . . .
As a result, I found I was being freed from . . .
and being freed for . . .

Friday ❖ 39th Day of Lent
"Forgiving and Reconciling"

Jesus said, "Father, forgive them, for they do not know what they are doing."
— Luke 23:34

Who am I not yet ready to forgive, and why?
For me to be free to forgive from my heart, I . . .

Saturday ❖ 40th Day of Lent
"Surrendering with Trust"

Do not let your hearts be troubled. Trust in God; trust also in me.
John 14:1

In what or whom do I place my deepest trust?
For me to trust unconditionally in God, I . . .

Epilogue
Easter Sunday

Jesus' journey to Jerusalem culminates in his resurrection from the dead. His resurrection is the fulfillment of the paschal mystery. It means that the process by which we experience life transformed comes in and through death. It is The Way and it is the only way transformation occurs.

For forty days we have moved through six weeks of time, all the while being drawn deeper by Love into a life of love for the sake of love.

In being companioned by the lives of Helen Keller, Dietrich Bonhoeffer, Simone Weil, Martin Luther King, Jr., Mother Teresa, and Jesus of Nazareth, we witnessed the importance of deep interior resolve and the consequences that come from a resolve steeped in grace and mystery. Most importantly, we appreciate the value of taking up our cross with the same motivation of love that Jesus took up his cross and to tend to the transforming cost of that love.

As our Lenten journey draws to a close, we realize we have accomplished nothing on our own. It has been done for us and to us. We are simply the recipients of amazing grace. The mystery of life transformed opens before us today. Let us rejoice and celebrate it in a moment of lingering silence, allowing the mystery of our life transformed to inform our heart and guide our continuing journey in whatever way it will.

Think of what is above, not of what is on earth.
For you have died, and your life is hidden with Christ in God.
Colossians 3:1-3

What we will be has not yet been made known.
But we know that when he appears,
we shall be like him, for we shall see him as he is.
1 John 3:2

END NOTES

[1] Luke 9:51. Scripture passages, unless otherwise noted, are taken from the *Jerusalem Bible*, Alexander Jones, General Editor, Doubleday and Company 1966.
[2] Luke 9:22
[3] Luke 9:23
[4] Matthew 10:38
[5] John 13:3
[6] John 3:8
[7] Luke 1:35
[8] Luke 2:39
[9] Luke 4:1
[10] John 3:34
[11] Robert Morris. "Riding the Wild Mountain Ox," *Weavings,* Volume XVI, number 4, p. 7.
[12] John 6:38
[13] John 4:34
[14] Matthew 12:50
[15] Matthew 7:21
[16] Matthew 26:42
[17] Bishop Desmond Tutu. "Allies of God," *Weavings,* Volume V, number 1, p. 40.
[18] Matthew 10:39
[19] Ephesians 4:22-24, *The Holy Bible*, New International Version. Zondervan Pub. House, 1994.
[20] Jeremiah 1:5
[21] Elaine M. Prevallet, SL. "Carrying in the Body the Death of Jesus," *Weavings,* Volume XVII, number 5, p. 24.
[22] Matthew 27:32
[23] James Finley. *Merton's Palace of Nowhere, 25th Anniversary Edition,* Ave Maria Press, 2003, p. 99.
[24] John 12:24
[25] Mary Ann Fatula, OP. "Current Trends: The Ministry of Reconciliation," *Spirituality Today,* Volume 40, number 2. p. 161.
[26] Matthew 6:15
[27] Luke 23:34

[28] Matthew 5:24
[29] Jean Blomquist. "Trusting Nimbly," *Weavings,* Volume V, number 3, p. 11.
[30] Luke 23:46
[31] John 14:1
[32] Hebrews 11:1, New International Version.
[33] John 13:34
[34] Anne Marie Drew. "Brave Emptiness: The Geography of Demons," *Weavings,* Volume VI, number 3, p. 32.
[35] Exodus 34:28
[36] Neibuhr, Richard. "Death of a Martyr," *Christianity and Crisis*, June 25, 1945, as quoted in Dietrich Bonhoeffer. *The Cost of Discipleship*. Touchstone: New York. 1995. pp.17-18.
[37] From Christian History Institute "Theologian Executed on Order of Hitler" *Glimpses,* Issue 63.
[38] "Farewell Address to Dexter Congregation." Nov. 29, 1959, Carson Clayborne, Ed. *The Autobiography of Martin Luther King, Jr.* New York: Warner Books. 1998. p. 136.
[39] Carson Clayborne, Ed. *The Autobiography of Martin Luther King, Jr.* New York: Warner Books. 1998. p. 136.